T0077966

WHY AMERICANS LIE AND THINK THEY CAN GET AWAY WITH IT

PAULETTE LEWIS-BROWN

authorHOUSE

AuthorHouse™
1663 Liberty Drive
Bloomington, IN 47403
www.authorhouse.com
Phone: 833-262-8899

Published by AuthorHouse 10/28/2020

ISBN: 978-1-7283-7348-5 (sc)
ISBN: 978-1-7283-7347-8 (e)

Print information available on the last page.

This book is printed on acid-free paper.

CHAPTER 1

While the World 🌍 is a big place.

America is a very small Country if you try to look into their abundance of lies. Why Americans lie is still a Banner flying high. With a Note written special to God. The fear of losing is America biggest fear. They fear the Invisible, they fear the unknown, yet their Faith is on the Front Burner, when in Reality it's really on the Back Burner. Americans worship Money 💵 they will Bribe the shirts off their own backs to win in any system. Americans Trust Money over Jesus.

They can see money, but they cannot see Jesus.

If you mention anything about the Voice of Jesus.

Americans will throw you under the Paranoid Bus
so fast, Then they would introduce one 🕎 of their
most powerful fake pill ✏ Lorazepam, Avian for
the Rich and Famous. America mental system is
a Sham, their Civil Rights and Justice System is
a lie, the True is always hidden somewhere, Jesus
have to step in on numerous occasions to free his
people in America.

Why Americans lie, still baffled me to this day.

As a born Jamaican We were told from a early stage
in life. Tell the TRUTH even if it kills US.

Gratitude 🙏 to my mother Sybil who plug ⚘ this note
in my head.

The truth will always set a Prisoner free in the World
even if it take a hundred years to free them.

If only Americans will know the Truth and believe

in the truth, they never look to President Donald

Trump for a lie.

The President is not in charge of our purple Hearts,

JESUS coats it's Red.♥.

Everyone knows the Truth when they're apart of

A lie. Find common sense on the corner of every

Brick house. It's the corner stone that the Builder

Rejected 🏚♂.

CHAPTER 2

When Americans lie, this makes them feel Powerful.

They lied in Groups, they have lies

For their Witnesses to follow, then they cover up their

Witnesses with triple lies for cover.

From the outer appearance it looks like the American

win, but most of their winnings are

with Abundance with lies.

When Crisis hits, their lies turns around

And hit them in their own heads. In the midst

Of it all, Americans will go hunting for some

Innocent underdog to Blame. They will even

Try to Bribe the underdog to lie on themselves.

Then the fake Credit hits the fan, American smile

And think they won.

When Americans lie, JESUS Piles up his notes

Then sends in his Warnings Quotes.

Leave my Angels alone is not insane. It's a

Poem when no one 🕯 takes the Blame.

When this Poets wants to call. JESUS is always

her Genius Invisible Wall. Born Jamaicans

Faith is always their first call. Truth is not a lie

And a lie could never be the truth.

Americans sees everyone from another Country as a

Spy. The pot thickens when they know that Aliens

have some common sense, Education or even a

Mountain ▲ of Wisdom.

An American will operate in Gangs in the Workplace,

sometimes asking Jesus for the FBI Instead of

Human Resource is like a poor man crying in vain. No one ✍ listens. Again Jesus steps in numerous times for the FBI behind the scenes, to protect his children.

Americans Documentations are mostly lies.

They lean to the side of policies and Protocols

Even though they never Follow the Safety rules.

We can only pray that in the Boiling point of every lies. Jesus innocent people will not get caught up in the Cross fire 🔥.

Pray for the World, but pray a special prayer for the Americans who believe that Money 💵 is the gold Spoon that all Aliens 👽 are after.

Pray for every lies told on a Foreigner, Multiply it by the abundance of Love given by our Heavenly Father. There's not an amount of Money that could

buy my Character, no man could fry me in their

bags of lies. JESUS knows the Truth.

Americans have to STOP 🤚 lying to be free.

Jamaicans have to acknowledge that Freedom is

Really Free. Fear not the born Americans, their lies

are a mere Painting 🖼 of the Unknown.

When an American lie, just give them a hug.

Tell them that they're never alone, because JESUS

knows the Truth, and he's on the Throne.

Never applied salt to a open wound.

Americans hurts like everyone else . They have feelings

too. They have been hurt by their Churches, Family

and even Friends. So When they're looking for

someone to take out their frustrations on. The

American always look for an Alien 👹 Maybe a born

Jamaican, or even an African . Trust God, Pray

and for Americans when they lie in Abundance.

The World will spin, then change will come, in the form of the TRUTH. COVID 19-5529 is not a Hoax. It's the Pyramid of lies boiled over to create a Fountain 👺. The World Discrimination Breach has hit the Ceiling. Panic and Chaos cannot work Together in a bag of lies. Americans fights to survive.

CHAPTER 3

Where are the true Americans

When you needed them, to protect you.

Where are the Police Force with their shields

To Block the Lies.

When we needed them in Crisis. Why do they hide.

Where's the Justice Department, Where's the Truth
　　in Civil Rights.

Will the Truth out weighs the lies, when you call in
　　the FBI.

Where's the Lawyer that will not lie for his clients

Where is the Judge ⚖ that will not accept Bribe

Where's the innocent Prisoners in America.

Let me answer, Behind Bars, While the liars are roaming the streets, looking for more innocent ones to defeat. Americans look in the mirror when you're looking for someone to blame for your Country Problems. Focus on the one ♨ in the Mirror then learn to love and accept everyone at the same Rate. Rich or Poor, open the Humanity door.

Where ever in the World Americans visit
Enjoy their moment in time. Their truth is Usually
Underline with a dose of lie, take it or leave it.
Life must go on. Give 100% Trust to Jesus let
Him divided it among men. Give freely from the
Heart ♥ expect nothing.

Keep on going, never give up, every Country Ancestors are always working. Jamaicans drive to survive is

at its peek. Love beyond Boundaries, Borders or Walls. Always tell the TRUTH.

Freedom to in America is still a question mark.

Gangs are in and out of the Workplace.

Politics is a lie. Safety can only be found in the Faith that sustain us. Never sell your Soul for the America Dollar 💲 it has no Value in Heaven.

Embrace all with this Motion. Love is the most

Dignified friend. The inner circle O is always what's within. The Circle is always open, but never broken. Search the World for Freedom it's

Always reaching for you as a Token.

America is the first Clue. Finding peace in a Ray

Of Sunshine ☀ will someday bring down the Rain ☁ with JESUS Rainbow 🌊 centered in your Frame 🖼.

CHAPTER 4

A message from An Angel.

My Hearts ❤ Bleeds when an American lies.

My Hearts ❤ Bleeds again when I read this to the World 🌍. Stop lying, Free innocent Jamaicans, from your cockAdoodleDo Sins.

Leave all Judgment to Jesus. His Freedom is Free.

Wave and think of the Invisible me with Wings.

Now when you think 💭 deeply

Look from within. I couldn't survive in the ordinary World so Father God created the Extraordinary one ☝So I can be me . So America you don't have

to Accommodate my Will. My Love lives in every

Household. It's called True Freedom.

Americans

Americans

The CODE 🔑

Is Love ♥.

To everyone who believes in Angels, don't stop.

Ancestors in the Grave, Still looking out for their

Love one's. America is in Turmoil and Pain.

Medication sales hits the Roof.

Doubts are everywhere, exhaustion is polluting

The Air. Invisible Covid-19-5529 can only be seen by

one 🕯 Angel 👼. Yet everyone is wearing a mask 😷.

Fake or Real Jesus sends Angels to look out for his

Angels on Earth.

I remember one of my 0400Am Dreams.

Wake up my beautiful Angel 👼, you used to

Count the Raindrops 🌧, but I used to count the

Sand on the Beach 🏖 with my Grandson.

Now this's no hassle, stay focus on SandCastle.

You will never go hungry from my family eyes.

Smile because when you look up in the Sky.

The Sun ☀ Will make you cry happy tears.

Someday you will Fly. Have no fear.

Circle O the World daily.

Spread your Wings.

Look out for poor man children

Trust them to be your friend.

See only the good in people.

Your Faith can only view things

That way. Jesus knows every

Heart ♥ give him all the opportunity

In the Judgment Zone.

Enjoy every happy and funny Bone

Smile with the Twists and Turns.

Focus on the important Tasks.

Leave Gossip alone.

Crisis is not a Dead End. It's a U turn

To start over again.

Live. Love ♥ and Laugh ☺.

In this World of Suspense.

Supreme will kicks in.

Success will stand Tall.

New friends will appears from

The middle of nowhere.🌍

Keep your eyes on Jesus

He's still your best friend to

The Very End. Angels are Real.

This's the Naked Truth.

Amen 🐏✍⬛

CHAPTER 5

We don't need to be in a Faith Gang to feel free.

All we really need is Jesus who always

Welcome 🔐 You and redeems me.

We don't need to be crucified for no reason

Jesus already died for our sins In all season.⛪

So open your Heart ♥ then look within

Jesus have Angels on Earth 🌍 with wings⊕

Lying won't cover the truth.

It only makes matters worst.

So it doesn't matter where in the World

We're from, it's free to hold the Bible in

Our right hand.

Telling the truth is not a Gift 🎁

It's a lesson learn from birth.

Every child needs a Father for a lift

Jesus protects those who were neglected

the most. 🌍

There's no pity Party here, with True Faith

There's nothing to fear.

Hope someday America will study the

Truth, Hope someday all Jamaicans Will

Study their ROOTS no need to lie in a foreign

Country, cause even when you give up Alien-ship

To be an American, Americans still see you as an

Alien that enters their Border to Freedom.

They only see money 💵 and if nothing is in it for

them, they wants nothing to do with it.

Then Americans will call in the Gangs, then leave out

the FBI until Road comes to an false Dead End.

Then Jesus steps in with his Abundance of Love and

TRUE FREEDOM. Wake up, look within.

This's no Hoax, to everyone reading 📖 this book.

Make the first move, and only tell the Truth.

Do it for Jesus, he has done so much for us.

Crisis, all Crisis will be washed away someday 🙏 😀.

Trust Jesus, Americans Trust Jesus . True Jamaicans,

trust only Jesus for guidance.

We're not helpless, we're just frightened with what

Americans can get away with, when they believe

No one ☝ is watching over an Alien.🙏

May God Bless all at the same Rate.

Someday, some sweet day.

AMEN 🙏 🔔

CHAPTER 6

When Lawyer Timothy Tack when up against invisible Jesus. He taught I wasn't smart enough to Represent myself, so he offered me $5000 to Disappear in thin Air, Jesus protects my every words, then he advised me to trust him.

My dearest Angel no need to take this Bribe money 💲 what they did to you on the Job is a Crisis, their lies that you Quit job is a Boiling point.

Give this book to the FBI. Expose their lies.

COVID-19-5529 ✚will come up again someday
6 Americans will have to Answer and square away.
The Truth will always prevail in the End.

Supervisors who saw you as a treat will someday apologize around the bend. CO-workers will look in the mirror and discipline themselves. There are Angels in the World who have the same Story, trusting Jesus in Every move is the smartest Domino in the World.

When Americans lie, and think they get away the Table turns and the World hits a Crisis Mode. 😬

A true win will not have Restrictions or Perimeters.

A true win will not Isolate the Truth.

Now that almost everyone in the World 🌍 can read. This book 📖 is a True Legacy of A born Jamaican Angel . Think Future is now.

Faith is the most important Factor in the World.

Family will always be there in daily prayers. 📖

Friends, true friends are hardest to find.

So Jesus chips in and sooth every soul. On one 🪑 accord. World Be loyal.

Lies have damage a lot of Family Trees.

Discrimination have broken every Rule in America.

Thank God for Jesus, or else even the Churches ⛪ Beliefs are Like broken records. Money 💲 is the Focus on the Pulpit.

Members are hungry and isolated . Smile 😊 and enjoy Jesus invisible blessings. Not everyone can afford to reveal it in Crisis.

Restrict, Isolation and execute will no longer work in America. Centra State Medical Center abuse this method. Someday it too will be a song.

Be happy, be Merry, Jesus is not Sleeping.

Believe me, he knows everything.

He's was my Lawyer and he always Win.

Anyone who wants to sue me for the Truth will have

to 'Sue Jesus'-with their lies.

My Right hand ✋ is on the Bible.

Father God is my only Judge.

I pray that no reader will get confused ♀ ♂when

They show gratitude 🙏 for the Sun ☀.

Release in the Air is pure Love ♥. Amen 🕊

AT THE END OF IT ALL
EVERY COUNTRY HAVE
LIARS. 🌍
BUT AMERICANS 🇺🇸 WON
THIS RACE WITH THEIR
MONEY 💵 AND POWER.
BUT DEEP IN THE HEART
OF A BORN JAMAICAN, 🇯🇲
IS A VERY POWERFUL NOTE
'JESUS ALWAYS HAVE THE
LAST LAUGH' 😂. 🙏 👍 PLB

Sorry America 🇺🇸

We really have to start
From Ground Zero.
Extreme liars in the Country
Is creating a Havoc and panic.
Show me your real Hammock
To weather the Storm 🌧️
Tell me the Truth to sustain
My Dignity. Give me a reason
Why I should forgive you.
Sorry America we have
Problems, let's hand ✋ them
to Jesus, only he alone can solve
Them. When you're looking for
Someone to lie, don't just blame
The President alone. Americans will lie
Just to create a fake face how to Win.
Then when false positive backfires
Innocent 😇 hearts got caught in the
Crossfire. Now look at COVID-19.
Sorry America, open your eyes
True love 🤍 never dies. ✖️
Americans, Stop lying, it's much cheaper.
Stop Crying. Faith is still standing to
heal every Family Tree. Be a Gatekeeper.
Let go and be Free. Sorry America
Truth must be told, let it begins with
Me. Jesus must be welcome in every
Household.

Find Peace within forever. Be Bold.
Let the World say, Sorry America
We're all coming in from the Cold.
Starting life over. If this makes you feeling
Any better, Scope every Country in the World
🌍 .
Father God Created liars. He loves
Everyone the same without shame.
And no, my Heavenly Father is not insane.
Read again, just this time SCREAM. 🤣 / .
WHY AMERICANS LIE AND THINK THEY
CAN GET AWAY WITH IT.?

When Jesus Created Angels

He knows that life would be

A challenge. To the unknown

Leave Jesus Angels Alone.

When Americans are up against invisible Jesus in the Justice system. Make it very clear that he's not sleeping behind the scene. He heard every lies and schemes.His Angels will only listen to his Voice. Accepting a Premature Bribe with Restrictions is like setting one self up with a False Positive to Win. Give away $5000 in the Future. Innocent people will not need an American Egotistical Lawyer from TAMPA to win. When they can hire Invisible Jesus through prayer. Just say out loud and Proud. WHY AMERICANS LIE AND THINK THEY CAN GET AWAY WITH IT.

Where are the Truth on Earth 🌎 Why should we Only look for it in HEAVEN.

DON'T LOOK BACK

YOU'RE NOT GOING

THAT WAY.

AMERICA LET US ALL

TELL THE TRUTH AND

MOVE FORWARD.

COVID-19 WILL BE A

THING OF THE PAST.

FAITH FOREVER WILL

LAST.

2021 WILL BE A TIME FOR HEALING

SO MANY DAMAGES TO THE HEART

OF MEN. FAMILIES ARE BROKEN DOWN

WITH CRISES AND LIES. HEALING WILL

BE FREE FOR EVERY SOUL. EVERY HEART

WILL BE AN OPEN BOOK

AROUND THE WORLD.

JESUS WILL HAVE FULL CONTROL IN ALL

CHURCHES AND WORKPLACE . SO MANY

AMERICANS WILL NOW ENJOY THEIR

OFFICES FROM HOME. HUSBANDS AND

WIVES WILL FINALLY FIND A MOMENT

TO CELEBRATE THEIR BOND. 2021 WILL

SMELL LIKE FREEDOM. COME HOME

ALL MY CHILDREN COME HOME.

JESUS IS CALLING ALL AMERICANS,

COME HOME, SEE ONLY THE TRUTH.

CALL IT AN ANTHEM. AMEN PLB

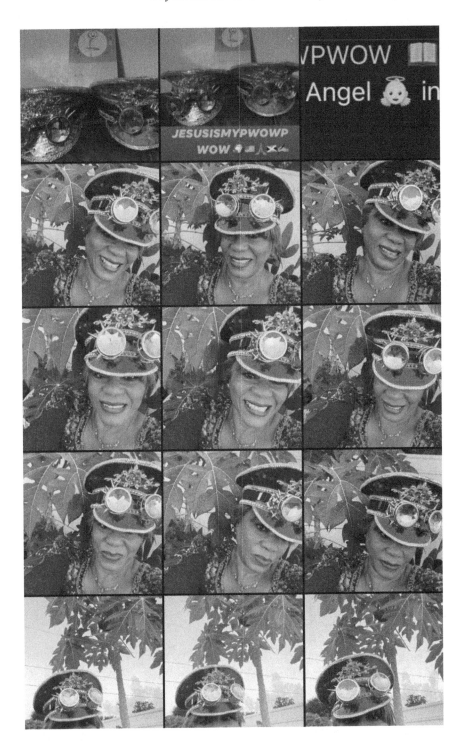

Printed in the United States
By Bookmasters